Thank You, Valued Customer, for Your Purchase of the "Artful Profanity"

We wanted to take a moment to express our heartfelt gratitude for choosing our "Artful Profan[...] us, and we're excited to have you as part of the InkXperiment family.

At InkXperiment, we're not just about coloring books; we're all about fostering creativity, imagination, and self-expression. Our coloring books are designed to take you on a journey of artistic exploration, allowing you to unleash your creativity and bring your own unique touch to every page.

InkXperiment Values:

1. Creativity: We believe that creativity is a powerful force that can inspire and uplift, and we aim to encourage it through our products.
2. Quality: We take pride in delivering high-quality coloring books that provide an enjoyable and stress-relieving experience.
3. Community: We cherish the vibrant community of artists and enthusiasts that our products have brought together, and we're excited to have you join us.

We would be delighted if you could take a moment to share your thoughts with us by leaving a review on our website. Your feedback helps us improve and ensures that we continue to offer products that bring joy and inspiration to all. And if you'd like to share pictures of your completed artwork, please do! We'd love to see the magical masterpieces you've created.

Your support means the world to us, and we're here to assist you with any questions or requests you may have. Feel free to reach out to us at via our Facebook page.

Once again, thank you for choosing InkXperiment. We can't wait to see the wonderful art you'll create with our "Artful Profanity."

Wishing you endless creativity and colorful moments,

Bfox
Owner /Designer
InkXperiment

P.S. Follow us on social media to stay updated on our latest releases, latest merch information, and more.

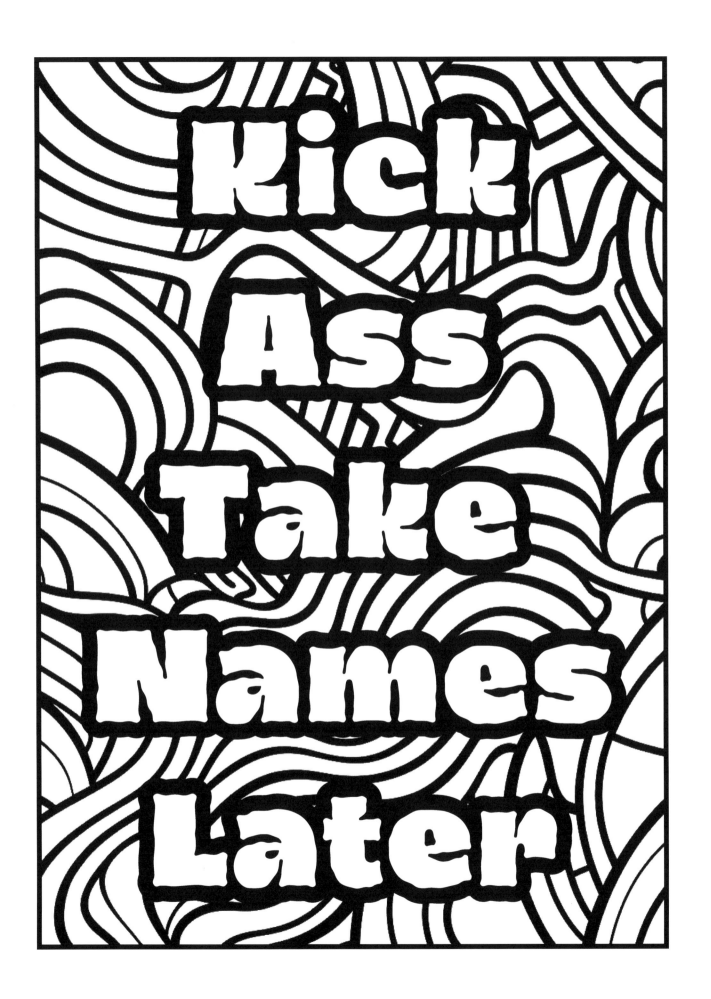

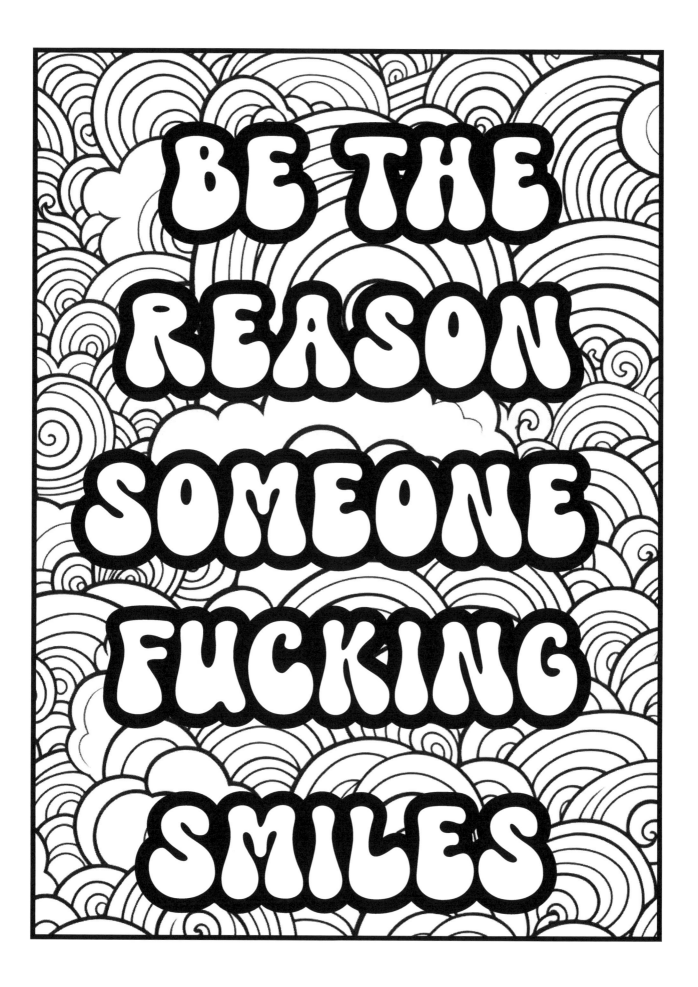

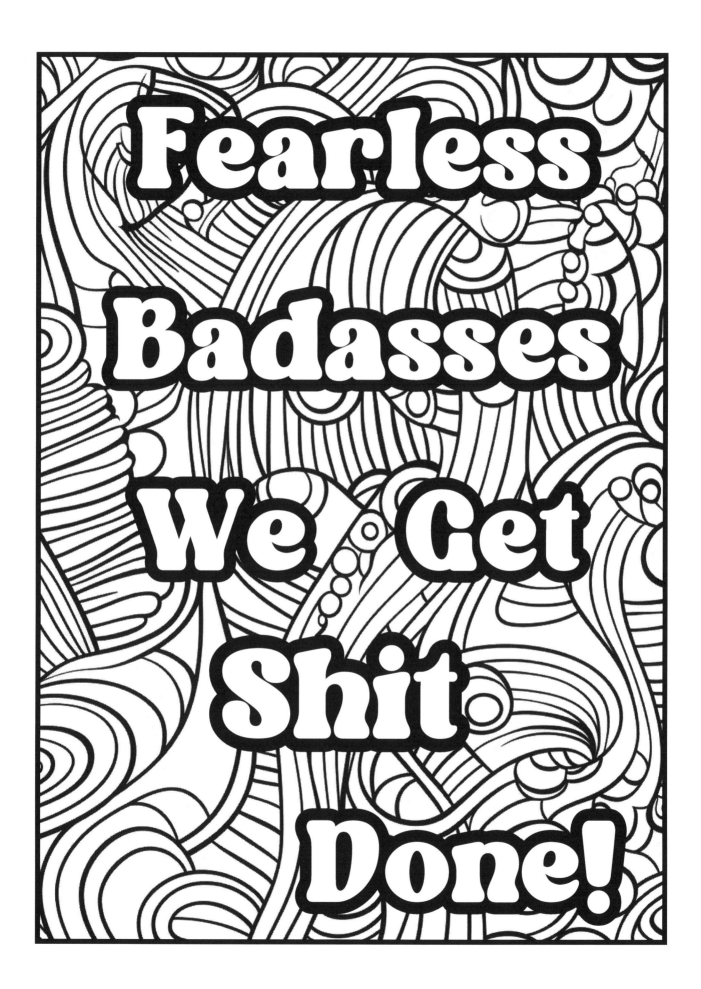

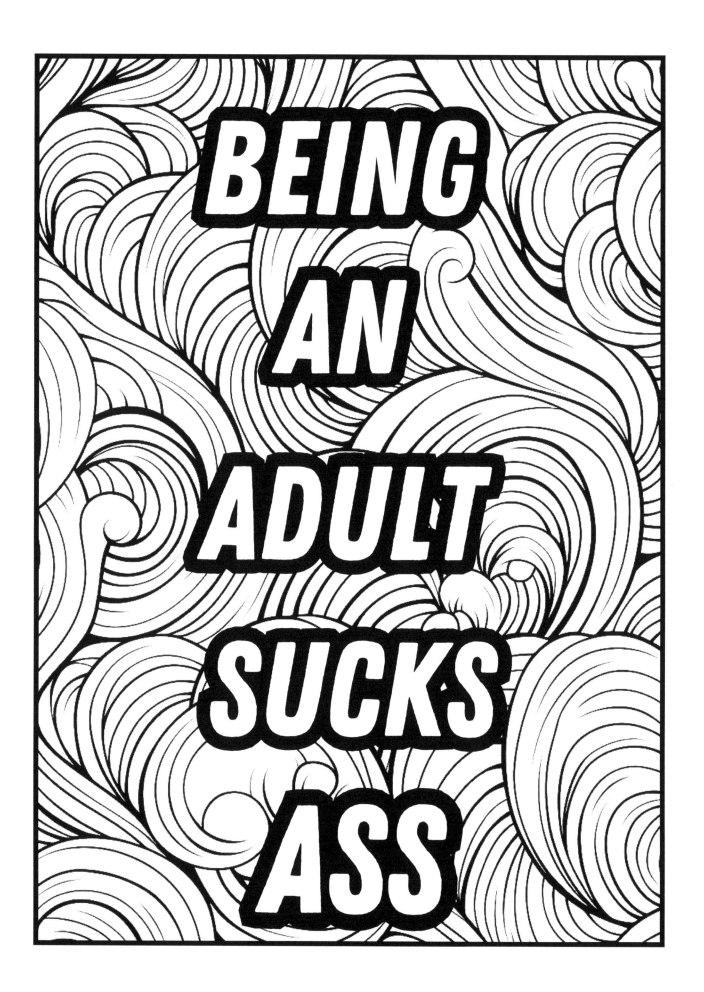

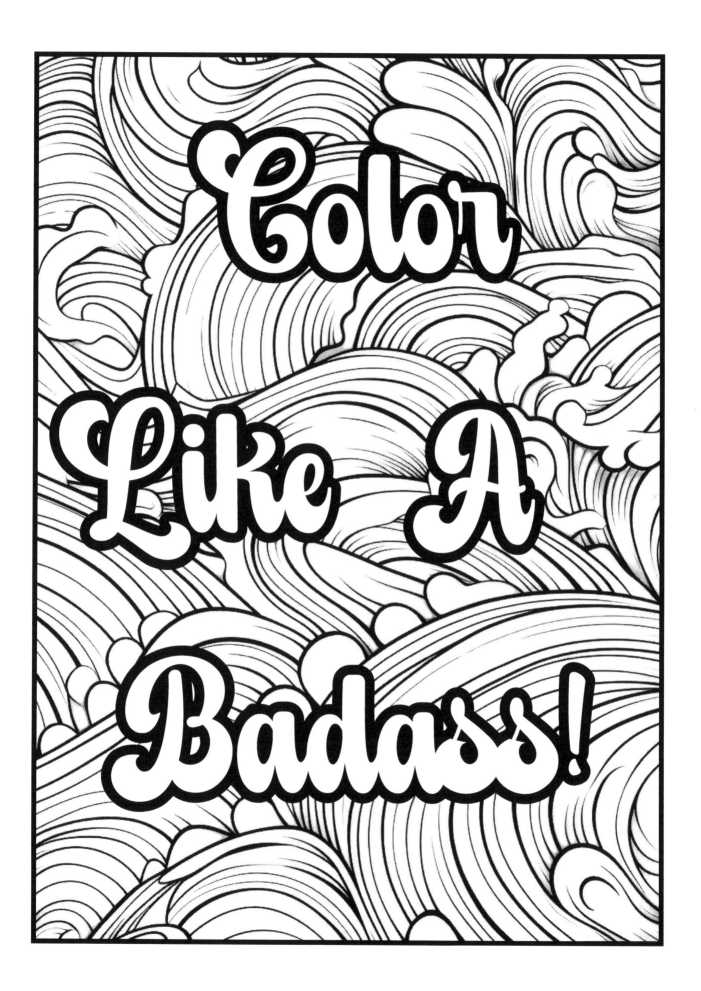

Made in United States
Troutdale, OR
03/20/2024

18607280R00060